Rebecca Austin Heath

Is there a need for reform within English Insider Dealing Laws

An analysis of the legal avenues of enforcement

Studies on International Business Law

Volume 1

Is there a need for reform within English Insider Dealing Laws

An analysis of the legal avenues of enforcement

by

Rebecca Austin Heath

SOCIETAS 2013

Bibliographic information published by the Deutsche Nationalbibliothek

The Deutsche Nationalbibliothek lists this publication in the Deutsche Nationalbibliografie; detailed bibliographic data are available in the Internet at http://dnb.dnb.de.

Bibliographische Information der Deutschen Nationalbibliothek

Die Deutsche Nationalbibliothek verzeichnet diese Publikation in der deutschen Nationalbibliographie; detaillierte bibliographische Daten sind im Internet über <http://dnb.ddb.de> abrufbar.

Societas Verlagsgesellschaft KG, Jena, 2013
Alle Rechte vorbehalten / All rights reserved

ISBN 978-3-944420-11-0

www.societas-verlag.de
www.societas-publishers.com

I would like to thank the Financial Services Authority for the useful information provided in compliance with a Freedom of Information request.

Table of Contents

Abbreviations 9
A. Introduction 11
B. Why should Insider Dealing be Prohibited? 15
    I.   Insider Dealing Provisions Under the Light of Economic Theory 16
    II.   The Impact of Insider Dealing 21
    III. Fairness, Morality and Social Ethics 23
    IV. Summarising Arguments 25
C. Public Enforcement 27
    I.   Analysis of the suitability of Public Enforcement Measures 28
        1. How The Criminal and Civil Enforcement Measures Protect Investors 28
            a) The Criminal Offence 29
            b) Criminal Procedure: Are Juries Appropriate in Insider Dealing Trials? 29
            c) The Insider as a Criminal and Insider Dealing as a Crime; a Criminological Perspective . 31
        2. Regulation as Alternative Approach 34
    II.   Identifying Specific Enforcement Issues 35
        1. Problem of Identification 35
        2. The Problem of Proof 37
        3. Civil Remedies and Public Enforcement 39
    III. Summarising Arguments for Section I: Public Enforcement 40

D.	**Private Enforcement**		41
	I.	Civil Remedies and Private Enforcement	42
		1. Implied rights of action Arising out of Insider Dealing provisions	42
		2. Alternative Rights of Action	43
		a) Financial Services Ombudsman	44
		b) Claims under Tort Law	45
		aa) Negligent Misstatement	45
		bb) The tort of Deceit	46
	II.	Analysing Equity's role	47
		1. Breach of Fiduciary duties	48
		2. Unjust Enrichment and Restitution	49
		3. Summarising Arguments for section II: Private enforcement	51
	III.	Concluding Thoughts and Possible suggestions for Reform; what can be proposed from the Above Arguments?	51
E.	**Reference List**		55
	I.	List of Cases	55
	II.	List of Statutes	57
	III.	Bibliography of Reference Sources	58

Abbreviations

EMH	Efficient Market Hypothesis.
EU	European Union.
FSA	Financial Services Authority.
FSMA 2000	Financial Services and Markets Act 2000 c.8.

A. Introduction

Those at the heart of corporations have, for centuries, unfairly profited from non-public information at the expense of others. The 'South Sea Bubble' of the 1720s, for example, saw 'massive amounts of insider dealing'[1] lead to, inter alia, 'the destruction of the wealth of Britain's richest'[2]. Yet, it is only within the last 22 years that the English law prohibited such action under Insider Dealing legislation; even at the beginning of the 20th century the courts in *Percival v. Wright* held that directors of a company were under no fiduciary duty to disclose information prior to purchase or sale of shares[3]. Insider Dealing first became an offence in the 1980s under the Companies Act 1980[4] and Companies Securities (Insider Dealing) Act 1985[5].

This original legislation was formed on the basis of the 'fiduciary theory'; i.e. the 'corporate fiduciary' duty was extended beyond the company, so that it was owed to the shareholders of the company[6]. This legislation was, therefore, said to protect the company[7]. The influence of the European Union ("EU") altered this outlook. It is the investors who 'are often at an informational disadvantage with respect

---

[1] J Davis, 'Secrets of Success: Look to the History for how the Bubble will burst' *The Independent* (London, 14 July 2004), p.15.

[2] P Beresford and M. Chittenden, 'Super-rich reel from Eur200bn slump; Wealth Even Britain's billionaires cannot escape the pain of the economic squeeze. Philip Beresford and Maurice Chittenden find the big losers' *The Sunday Times* (London, 28 December 2008), p.7.

[3] *Percival v. Wright* [1902] 2 Ch. 421.

[4] Companies Act 1980 c.22, Part V.

[5] Company Securities (Insider Dealing) Act 1985 c.8.

[6] A F Loke, 'From the fiduciary theory to information abuse: the changing fabric of Insider Trading law in the U.K., Australia and Singapore' (2006) 54(1). The American Journal of Comparative Law, 123.

[7] P L Davies, 'The European Community's Directive on Insider Dealing: From Company Law to Securities Markets Regulation' [1991] Oxford J. Legal Stud. 92.

to issuers of securities'[8], and so modern Insider Dealing provisions govern the relationships in the securities markets, with the primary aim being protection of investors and potential investors of a company[9]; the EU council directive on 'coordinating regulations on insider dealing'[10] explicitly stated that insider dealing provisions should protect investors 'against the improper use of inside information'[11]. Thus it has been stated that English Insider Dealing laws have shifted from a 'company law approach'[12], based on the fiduciary relationship and protection of the company, to a 'securities markets approach'[13], based on protection of the capital markets and investors[14].

This dissertation will analyse the relevant enforcement methods available under English Insider Dealing laws, asking how they can be developed to meet the aim of investor protection[15]. It will first discuss the rationale behind the regulation of Insider Dealing, arguing for reformation of the law rather than abolishment. Section I will then analyse the public enforcement of Insider Dealing under English law, looking at enforcement through the FSA, as the UK's main investigatory body and prosecutor. It will analyse both the criminal and civil offence; held under Part V Criminal Justice Act 1993 and Part VIII Financial Services and Markets Act 2000 ("FSMA 2000") respectively. Section II examines the public enforcement mechanisms available to the investor, delving into both the civil law and equitable principles. This dissertation will then conclude by providing a summary of the

---

[8]F Allen and R Herring, 'Banking Regulation versus Securities Market Regulation' (2001) The Wharton Financial Institutions Center, University of Pensylvania, 1, 22-3.

[9]For this reason, this dissertation will focus on protection of investors when analysing enforcement methods.

[10]The Council of European Communities, *'Coordinating regulations on Insider Dealing'* Council Directive 89/592/EEC. Available at: http://www.esma.europa.eu/system/files/Dir_89_592.PDF (last accessed; 07/09/12).

[11]Ibid.

[12]P L Davies, 'The European Community's Directive on Insider Dealing: From Company Law to Securities Markets Regulation' [1991] Oxford J. Legal Stud. 92, 92.

[13]Ibid.

[14]Ibid.

[15]It has been stated that an 'analysis of the insider dealing and market manipulation regimes that have emerged in the UK and the rest of the EU is truly urgent'; E. E. Avgouleas, *'The Mechanics and Regulation of Market Abuse: A Legal and Economic Analysis'* (2005, Oxford University Press), 6. This dissertation aims to provide this through developing the existing academic analysis in this area.

analysis given, with suggested solutions to the issues discussed, thus highlighting possibilities for reform.

B. Why should Insider Dealing be Prohibited?

The courts rarely get involved in financial transactions and corporate dealings; commerce is intended to be a free market. In other words the majority of commercial dealings are free from regulation. The principle idea behind a free market economy is that it builds competition and encourages innovation, as markets are controlled by supply and demand; where there is a need for a particular commodity, the market will supply it[16]. Thus the law will only intervene when the circumstances justify regulation[17].

Insider dealing has been recognised as one of these circumstances, and Cheffins went as far to say that:

> '*a country will develop a vibrant stock market and a widely dispersed pattern of share ownership only if its legal system regulates insider opportunism*'. [18]

Despite this, many academics have argued for the legalisation of Insider Dealing and it is this debate which is the focus of this chapter. The ongoing debate falls under three general branches: (1) economic theoretical analysis; (2) whether or not the impact Insider Dealing has on the victim is truly harmful and (3) social welfare.

---

[16] A H Shand, '*Free Market Morality: The Political economy of the Austrian School*' (1990 Routledge), 199.

[17] J Dine, '*The Comprehensive Review of Company Law: the Consultative Document*' (1998) 19(3) Comp. Law, 82, 84.

[18] B R Cheffins, '*Does the Law Matter? The Separation of Ownership and Control in the United Kingdom*' (2001) 30 J. Legal. Stud, 459, 465.

B. Why should Insider Dealing be Prohibited?

I. Insider Dealing Provisions Under the Light of Economic Theory

The prohibition of Insider Dealing has been the topic of a long standing economic debate; arguments for legalisation centre on Fama's 'Efficient Capital Market Theory'[19], also known as the 'Efficient Market Hypothesis' ("EMH"). Fama's theory argues that the market is 'informationally efficient'[20] when share valuations accurately reflect all relevant information[21]. This information must be made public before it can be incorporated into the market price, and so the market is 'informationally efficient' when all information pertaining to shares is public. Fama classified markets into weak, semi-strong or strong forms: in weak forms only historical information is available; in semi-strong forms some information is public and some is private, the price must adapt quickly as new information is made public; and in strong forms all information relevant to the securities is publicly available[22] (see 'Table 1' below). Once public information is incorporated into the market price it is described as being 'stale'[23], meaning it is no longer profitable. If the strong form stands and all information is incorporated into the market price, and is thereby stale, it is impossible for insiders to make a profit on non-public information and thereby 'beat the market'[24]. It would, therefore, seem logical that the theory supported the regulation of Insider Dealing.

---

[19] E F Fama, *'Efficient Capital Markets: a Review of Theory and Empirical Work'* (1970) 25(2) Journal of Finance, 383.

[20] S J Grossman and J. E. Stiglitz, *'On the Impossibility of Informationally Efficient Markets'* (1980) 70(3) American Economic Review, 393.

[21] E F Fama, *'Efficient Capital Markets: a Review of Theory and Empirical Work'* (1970) 25(2) Journal of Finance, 383, 383.

[22] E F Fama, *'Efficient Capital Markets: a Review of Theory and Empirical Work'* (1970) 25(2) Journal of Finance, 383, 383 and 388; E E Avgouleas, 'The Mechanics and Regulation of Market Abuse: A Legal and Economic Analysis' (2005, Oxford University Press), 45-6.

[23] A Shleifer, *'Inefficient Markets: an Introduction to Behavioural Finance'* (2000, Oxford University Press), 5.

[24] L A Stout, *'The Mechanisms of Market Inefficiency: an Introduction to New Finance'* (2003) 28(4) Journal of Corporation Law, 635, 640.

I. Insider Dealing Provisions Under the Light of Economic Theory 17

Table 1: Fama's Efficient Market Hypothesis summary.

	Stale information (i.e. information incorporated into the market price)	How this translates to efficiency
Strong form.	All information.	All information is incorporated into the securities' price, so rational investment decisions may be made[25]. Thus the market is considered efficient.
Semi-strong form.	Public information only.	Market prices are based only on the information that is public. As some information is non-public, this model is not as efficient as the strong form. However it is the preferred model, as the strong model is not practical.
Weak form.	Historical information only.	Valuations are based on past prices only. This makes the market unpredictable[26] and so it is less efficient.

However, the theory accepts that the 'strong form'is'not strictly valid'[27]; in reality information does not leak so quickly that there will never be opportunities for individuals to engage in insider dealing[28]. Moreover, some information is commercially sensitive, particularly with new technological information that gives the owner a clear commercial advantage; to require public access to such information defeats the competitive incentive and degrades a company's individuality[29]. Therefore,

---

[25] E F Fama, *'Efficient Capital Markets: a Review of Theory and Empirical Work'* (1970) 25(2) Journal of Finance, 383,383.
[26] A Shleifer, *'Inefficient Markets: an Introduction to Behavioural Finance'* (2000, Oxford University Press), 6.
[27] E F Fama, *'Efficient Capital Markets: a Review of Theory and Empirical Work'* (1970) 25(2) Journal of Finance, 383, 410.
[28] 'The insider traders occupying minimum security prisons for making illegal profits themselves represent some evidence against the strong form EMG'; A Shleifer, *'Inefficient Markets: an Introduction to Behavioural Finance'* (2000, Oxford University Press), 6-7.
[29] For a more detailed discussion on the conflict between the transparency of securities markets and confidentiality see; S Gilotta, *'Disclosure in Securities Markets*

it is generally accepted that the semi-strong model is ideal[30], under which markets are considered efficient when prices do not reflect inside information. In this sense this model facilitates Insider Dealing. It should be noted, however, that facilitating Insider Dealing is very different from arguing for the legalisation of the offence; the semi-strong model simply gives an individual the opportunity to illegally trade, but it is still considered an offence to act upon that opportunity.

The economic arguments for the legalisation of Insider Dealing arise out of the concept of 'fundamental value efficiency'[31]; a market is 'fundamental value efficient' where prices 'mirror the best possible estimates... of the actual economic values'[32], and so while it may be accepted that capital markets demonstrate informational efficiency even with inside information being held privately, it does not follow that the market has fundamental value efficiency. This is different from informational efficiency, which is concerned with the share valuation's reflection of relevant information rather than the share valuation's reflection of its economic value[33].

Share valuations are reflective of their demand, which allows traders to 'infer non-public information from transitory price fluctuations or from the source of trades'[34]. Thus a share's valuation represents the position of traders' as a collective group. According to EMH theory, investors analyse and base their decisions on this[35]; known as 'price and trade decoding activity'[36].

---

and the Firm's Need for Confidentiality: Theoretical Framework and Regulatory Analysis' (2012) 13(1) E.B.O.R., 45.

[30] E F Fama, 'Efficient Capital Markets: II' (1991) 46(5) Journal of Finance, 1575.

[31] L A Stout, 'Are Stock Markets Costly Casinos? Disagreement, Market Failure, and Securities Regulation' (1995) 81(3) Va. L. Rev, 611.

[32] L A Stout, 'The Mechanisms of Market Inefficiency: an Introduction to New Finance' (2003) 28(4) Journal of Corporation Law, 635, 640.

[33] L A Stout, 'Are Stock Markets Costly Casinos? Disagreement, Market Failure, and Securities Regulation' (1995) 81(3) Va. L. Rev, 611, 646-7.

[34] E E Avgouleas, 'The Mechanics and Regulation of Market Abuse: A Legal and Economic Analysis' (2005, Oxford University Press), 80-1; H S Houthakker and P J Williamson, 'The Economics of Financial Markets' (1996, Oxford University Press), 290.

[35] E E Avgouleas, 'The Mechanics and Regulation of Market Abuse: A Legal and Economic Analysis' (2005, Oxford University Press), 80.

[36] E E Avgouleas, 'The Mechanics and Regulation of Market Abuse: A Legal and Economic Analysis' (2005, Oxford University Press), 80-1; H S Houthakker and P. J. Williamson, 'The Economics of Financial Markets' (1996, Oxford University Press), 290.

On this basis, allowing insiders to trade would give investors a better opportunity to infer non-public information, and thus the commercially sensitive information would be incorporated into the market without the confidential content being divulged. Using 'price and trade decoding activity'[37], investors will interpret the fundamental value of the shares and 'respond to the new information by bidding up prices when the news is good and bidding them down when the news is bad'[38]. As the 'demand for securities determines prices'[39], the insiders' trades, plus possible further trade from investors'[40], will bring the price 'closer to what it would have been had the information been disclosed'[41]; thus enhancing the 'fundamental value efficiency' of the capital market (see 'Figure 1' below). For this reason, some economists argue that Insider Dealing should be legalised.

---

[37] Ibid.

[38] A Shleifer, *'Inefficient Markets: an Introduction to Behavioural Finance'* (2000, Oxford University Press), 2.

[39] E E Avgouleas, *'The Mechanics and Regulation of Market Abuse: A Legal and Economic Analysis'* (2005, Oxford University Press), 80.

[40] As investors analyse the market and their confidence in the stock either grows or diminishes.

[41] D W Carlton and D R Fischel, *'The Regulation of Insider Trading'* (1993) 35(5) Stanford Law Review, 857, 868.

B. Why should Insider Dealing be Prohibited?

Figure 1: the Valuation of Shares.

```
                    ┌─────────────────┐
                    │  Share prices   │
                    │ illustrate the  │
                    │position of traders.│
                    └─────────────────┘
                   ↗                   ↘
    ┌──────────────────┐         ┌──────────────────┐
    │ This alteration in│         │ Investors analyse│
    │  price brings the │         │  this and either │
    │ shares closer to  │         │  invest or do not│
    │ their fundamental │         │  invest in shares│
    │      value.       │         │    depending on  │
    └──────────────────┘         │whether the news is│
             ↑                    │   good or bad.   │
             │                    └──────────────────┘
    ┌──────────────────┐                   ↓
    │ This increase or │         ┌──────────────────┐
    │ decrease alters  │         │                  │
    │  the price of the│ ←────── │  Trade either    │
    │securities; 'demand│        │  increases or    │
    │ for securities   │         │   decreases.     │
    │determines price' │         │                  │
    │(see footnnote 21)│         └──────────────────┘
    └──────────────────┘
```

The EMH does not, however, explain market bubbles; a term which refers to 'large market changes and excessive volatility (booms and busts)'[42]. Initially stock markets demonstrate a rise, invigorating investors and creating a positive hysteria, described as a 'euphoric noise'[43]. This euphoria allows for inside deals to go unnoticed and leads to a 'pervasive decline in market ethics'[44], so that even when insider's deals are noticed, their behaviour is overlooked because of the rose-tinted glasses worn by market players. This environment created by bubbles, thereby, facilitates insider deals. This gap in the EMH is, therefore, particularly problematic for this discussion.

---

[42] L Gullifer and J Payne, *'Corporate Finance Law: Principles and Policy'* (2011, Hart Publishing Ltd), 456.

[43] E E Avgouleas, *'The Mechanics and Regulation of Market Abuse: A Legal and Economic Analysis'* (2005, Oxford University Press), 89.

[44] Ibid.

Bubbles can be explained by Behavioural Finance theories, i.e. studies of investors' cognitive behaviour. Behavioural finance goes some way to explaining investor's decision making process, which is generally based on one or more of the following[45]: (1) bounded rationality, a term used to describe an investor's 'limited ability to receive and process information'[46]; (2) overconfidence, or in other words investor's optimism in the market[47]; (3) 'heuristic-driven bias'[48], i.e. investors rely on 'rules of thumb'[49] and past experiences; and (4) 'herding', which refers to the trends formed from previous investors decisions. These trends then get followed by other investors[50]. According to Behavioural Finance theory, bubbles are caused by investors displaying one or more of the above behaviours, and thus displaying what is termed irrational behaviour; this contradicts the main argument put forward by EMH theory, which is based on the premise of investors rationally analysing market patterns.

Investors' decisions are cognitively complex and unpredictable; decisions are based on more fluid concepts such as overconfidence. As such, investors' decisions are not based on an analysis of the market as the EMH suggests (see figure 1), and thus legalising Insider Dealing would not enhance the 'fundamental value efficiency' of capital markets. Thus Behavioural Finance findings pose a serious threat to the argument for the legalisation of Insider Dealing outlined above.

II. The Impact of Insider Dealing

Manne described Insider Dealing as a 'victimless crime'[51], and many academics have since argued that because Insider Dealing does not

---

[45] A detailed analysis of these theories is outside the scope of this dissertation. For such detailed analysis please see the referenced material below; footnote [46] - footnote [50].

[46] E E Avgouleas, 'The Mechanics and Regulation of Market Abuse: A Legal and Economic Analysis' (2005, Oxford University Press), 65.

[47] For how investor overconfidence effects the capital market see; R J Shiller, 'Measuring Bubble Expectations and Investor Confidence' (2000) 1(1) Journal of Psychology and Financial Markets, Financial Markets, 49.

[48] H Shefrin, 'Beyond Greed and Fear: Understanding Behavioural Finance and the Psychology of Investing' (2002, Oxford University Press).

[49] Ibid, 4.

[50] E E Avgouleas, 'The Mechanics and Regulation of Market Abuse: A Legal and Economic Analysis' (2005, Oxford University Press), 68-73.

[51] H G Manne, 'Insider Trading and Proprietary Rights in New Information' (1985) 4(3) Cato Journal, 933.

harm individuals, it should not be illegal. The argument is based on the premise that the 'victims' of insider trades would have traded even if the insider had not bought/sold the shares. Investment transactions are normally conducted through third parties; stock brokers, for example, act on behalf of the investor[52]. Rarely will investors purchase the shares themselves, and so they have limited control in the purchase price; while the third party will try to procure the best deal for the investor, whom they are acting for, they will work to a bottom or top line (depending on whether they are buying or selling)[53]. The investor was willing to trade at that bottom or top line price regardless.

Moreover, the majority of transactions are completed through electronic order book systems, such as the Stock Exchange Trading Service (SET)[54], which match buyers with sellers automatically. Thus, if the investor in question had not purchased the shares, they would have been automatically allocated to another willing investor. The insider therefore caused the investor no harm[55]; if the stock market experiences a fluctuation as a result of the inside trade, the investor could even benefit from the transaction.

This argument is, however, fundamentally flawed and has been met with much criticism. It is clear that the investor suffered an economic loss through the trade and this loss was distinct from the kind of loss 'suffered in equally informed transactions'[56]. The investor has suffered a loss of opportunity; either an opportunity to sell for a higher price or buy at a lower price. The loss suffered by a victim of insider dealing, and the distinction between this loss and the kind of loss suffered by poor choice of investment, provides sufficient justification for the regulation of Insider Dealing. This assertion has recently been given judicial approval in *R v. Christopher McQuoid*[57].

---

[52] S Griffin, *'Company Law; Fundamental Principles'* (3rd Ed. 2000, Pearson Education Limited), 178-80.

[53] Ibid.

[54] http://www.londonstockexchange.com/products-and-services/trading-services/guidetotradingservices.pdf (last accessed: 30/08/12).

[55] H G Manne, *'Insider Trading and Proprietary Rights in New Information'* (1985) 4(3) Cato Journal, 933, 934.

[56] I B Lee, *'Fairness and Insider Trading'* (2002) 1 Colum. Bus. L. Rev, 119, 160.

[57] [2010] 1 Cr. App.R. (S.) 43, per Lord Judge CJ, at [271].

III. Fairness, Morality and Social Ethics

It has been argued that Insider Dealing should be prohibited simply because it is unfair or immoral[58]. This argument is similar to that which is put forward by Fair Play theory, which states that each member of society 'enjoys the benefit of the co-operative enterprise, [and] each is obliged to co-operate in accordance with the rules' imposed by the law[59]. This creates, what is assumed to be, an equal balance of benefits and burdens and, where an individual benefits 'from the protection of the law whilst failing to restrain himself in accordance with its demands, [(s)he] free-rides on the system of co-operation'[60], and the balance is disrupted. This disruption is deemed a moral justification for punishment, as the offender is not 'playing fair'.

Under the fairness argument Insider Dealing is classed as either a breach of duty or a form of fraud[61], and is likened to the unfair advantage an athlete gains from taking performance enhancing drugs:

> '*A clean athlete deserves her success, whereas the doped athlete does not. It is this species of ethical argument which distinguishes the acceptability of a well-resourced, skillful and dedicated investment firm relying on their superior analysts to make excellent predictions about market movements and so to make money from counterparties, from the unacceptability of someone exploiting an unfair advantage acquired through misuse of inside information to make a profit from dealing with counterparties before the market has had time to react to the information or even to know about the information. The former dealer deserves their profit whereas the latter does not.*'[62]

Insider Dealing is viewed as cheating both the investor who falls victim and the securities market itself. The fact that Insider Dealing cheats the securities market presents an additional harm to the harm

---

[58] For example; I B Lee, '*Fairness and Insider Trading*' (2002) 1 Colum. Bus. L. Rev, 119.
[59] M Matravers, '*Justice and Punishment: The rationale of Coercion*' (2003, Oxford Scholarship Online), 54.
[60] Ibid.
[61] S P Green, '*Cheating*' (2004) 23(2) Law & Phil, 135, 178-81.
[62] A Hudson, '*The Law of Finance*' (2009, Thomson Reuters (Legal) Limited), 328.

caused to the investor, which is described above. This harm 'might be construed as one of destablising society's processes of property and financial transfers'[63]. In this sense, the securities market is also a victim in Insider Dealing cases; adding a further dimension to the arguments explored in the previous section.

The fairness argument has been criticised for lack of content, as the concept of fairness is difficult to define, and consequently it is hard to state exactly why Insider Dealing is unfair[64]. Lee stated that 'fairness could mean many things'[65], and it often means something slightly different to each individual. Academics have attempted to define the concept of fairness in securities markets. For example, Lee suggested 'the rule against coercion', 'dishonesty' and 'the convention of promise-keeping'[66] are all examples of 'a rule of fairness'[67]. Although these definitions are true to the meaning of fairness, they are fairly generic; they do not specifically explain why Insider Dealing is unfair. It is also difficult to define the scope of the fairness argument. There are many industries which thrive on the basis that one party is able to profit from knowledge unknown to another, and it is difficult to expressly define when this use of knowledge is fair or unfair[68]. The concept of fairness is, therefore, vague in both definition and scope, and while practically it is clear that there is a need for fairness in order for the securities markets to run effectively, on an academic level this argument is difficult to rely on.

A stronger argument for the prohibition of Insider Dealing is the assumed benefit prohibition has on both society and, more specifically, the markets[69]. Arguably information is synonymous with power, and thus allowing insiders to trade on the basis of their non-public information would give them an unjustifiable power over capital markets. Insiders would 'have a strong incentive to manipulate the timing and

---

[63]D Ormerod, *'The Fraud Act - Criminalising Lying?'* [2007] Crim. L.R., 193, 196.

[64]F H Easterbrook, *'Insider Trading, Secret Agents, Evidentiary Privileges and the Production of Information'* [1981] Supt. Ct. Rev, 309, 323-330

[65]I B Lee, *'Fairness and Insider Trading'* (2002) 1 Colum. Bus. L. Rev, 119, 141.

[66]Ibid, 147-148.

[67]Ibid, 147.

[68]F H Easterbrook, *'Insider Trading, Secret Agents, Evidentiary Privileges and the Production of Information'* [1981] Supt. Ct. Rev, 309, 324.

[69]This is closely related to the aim of Insider Dealing provisions, described in the introduction.

quality of disclosure of corporate information in order to exploit their trading advantage over outside investors'[70]. Not only would this create an unpredictable and uneven playing ground for investors, it would also lead to a severe lack of investor confidence in the capital market.

In order to encourage investor confidence, the market must be 'seen to be fair and no one should be seen to be at a disadvantage'[71]. Investor confidence is of paramount importance to the world of business; without it investors 'are likely to stop investing in securities markets because they will consider that those markets are rigged in favour of insiders. Consequently, there will be a drying-up of liquidity for companies... wishing to access capital markets'[72]. In regulating the conduct of market players, the law gives investors some comfort in knowing they have a right of action if the investor makes a loss because the seller traded on the basis of non-public information. This is incredibly important for the growth of the economy, as 'financial markets thrive or decline depending on the level of confidence investors have in them'[73].

IV. Summarising Arguments

In this chapter, it has been suggested that: (a) economic arguments for the legalisation of Insider Dealing are fairly weak, as they lack an understanding of the complexity of investor behavior; (b) the harm caused by Insider Dealing justifies its regulation, and (c) Insider Dealing regulations are necessary for both social and economic reasons. Financial markets are incredibly volatile, booms and busts are fairly frequent, and, as discussed above, insider deals thrive in this instability. Hudson stated that:

'once a century there comes a financial crisis so great that it causes everyone to question whether our arrangements

---

[70] E E Avgouleas, *'The Mechanics and Regulation of Market Abuse: A Legal and Economic Analysis'* (2005, Oxford University Press), 97.

[71] P Barnes, *'Insider Dealing and Market Abuse: the UKs Record on Enforcement'* [2010] MPRA Paper No. 25585: http://mpra.ub.uni-muenchen.de/25585/ (last accessed: 20/08/12), 4.

[72] A Hudson, *'The Law of Finance'* (2009, Thomson Reuters (Legal) Limited), 326.

[73] E E Avgouleas, *'The Mechanics and Regulation of Market Abuse: A Legal and Economic Analysis'* (2005, Oxford University Press), 18.

B. Why should Insider Dealing be Prohibited?

for organising the financial system are adequate or even sensible'[74].

Although the current economic situation originated from financial markets within banking, capital markets have, and will continue to, complement the banks[75]. It has been stated that 'well-functioning markets are essential for banks to be sufficiently well-capitalised to expand credit availability to borrowers without increasing the risk of the banking system beyond prudent levels'[76]. Increasing investor confidence would, therefore, be incredibly beneficial in the current climate. The European Union ("EU") has recently taken this view and has suggested proposals to better harmonise Insider Dealing provisions across Member States[77]. For this and the above reasons, this dissertation will now focus on the available enforcement mechanisms; looking where the law may need reform.

---

[74] A Hudson, *'The Law of Finance'* (2009, Thomson Reuters (Legal) Limited), 830.

[75] F Song and A V Thakor, *'Financial System Architecture and the Co-Evolution of Banks and Capital Markets'* (2010) 120(547), 1021, 1023.

[76] F Song and A Thakor, *'Banks and Capital Markets as a Coevolving Financial System'* [2010] Vox: http://www.voxeu.org/article/banks-and-capital-markets-coevolving-financial-system (last accessed; 20/08/12).

[77] T Edmonds, *'Market Abuse Directive'*, House of Commons Library Publications, 15 June 2012.

C. Public Enforcement

There are a number of ways in which the FSA, as the UK's main public enforcement body, can enforce Insider Dealing provisions. Firstly, the FSA could initiate criminal proceedings against the offenders under s.52 Criminal Justice Act 1993. Under this provision a person who has connections within a company, either through employment, directorship, share ownership or a contact, is criminally liable for insider dealing where (s)he: (1) deals in 'price-affected securities'[78] using specific and non-public information about the securities in question which, if made public, would 'be likely to have a significant effect on the price of any securities'[79]; (2) 'encourages another person to deal in securities' using such information as described in (1)[80]; or (3) discloses such information as described in (1) to an outsider, and as such tips the outsider of the opportunity[81].

Alternatively the FSA could exercise the powers given under (a) s.123 FSMA 2000, and impose a civil penalty, or (b) s.383 FSMA 2000, and apply for restitutionary damages on behalf of the victim. The civil offence under the FSMA 2000 is fairly similar; encompassing both the offences previously described in (1) and (3)[82]. However, it also includes a wider reaching offence: 'where the behaviour... (a) is based on information which is not generally available to those using the market but which if available to a regular user of the market, would be, or would be likely to be, regarded by him as relevant when deciding the terms on which transactions in qualifying investments should be effected, and (b) is likely to be regarded by a regular user of the market as a fail-

---

[78] Criminal Justice Act 1993 c.36, s.52(1).
[79] Ibid, s. 56(1).
[80] Ibid, s.52(2)(a).
[81] Ibid, s.52(2)(b).
[82] Financial Services and Markets Act 2000 c.8, s. 118 (2) and (3).

ure on the part of the person concerned to observe the standard of behaviour reasonably expected of a person in his position in relation to the market'[83].

The criminal and civil offences are only effective, however, when they can be sufficiently enforced. This section analyses the public enforcement of Insider Dealing, asking if the criminal and civil offences enforcement measures are both suitable and appropriate, and analysing specific enforcement issues.

I. Analysis of the suitability of Public Enforcement Measures

Public enforcement of the offence of Insider Dealing comprises of both criminal and civil measures. This chapter looks at these measures, analysing (a) whether the civil and criminal measures combined sufficiently protect investors and (b) the suitability of criminal sanctions and how criminal enforcement measures can be strengthened. It will conclude by asking if regulation of the offence is more appropriate than the current public enforcement methods; looking at the necessity of public enforcement.

1. How The Criminal and Civil Enforcement Measures Protect Investors

Protection of investors has been highlighted as one of the aims of Insider Dealing laws, and the significance of protecting investors has been explained in chapter one. At first glance, public enforcement of Insider Dealing may not seem to achieve this aim; the criminal and civil offences of Insider Dealing in the UK do not necessarily take the investor's interests into account, the objective being punishment of the insider and deterrence, 'not the recovery of the...funds for the victim'[84]. In this sense, it would seem the public enforcement measures focus on protection of the capital markets rather than investors. Protection of investors and protecting the integrity of the market are, however, interlinked[85]; if

---

[83] Ibid, s.118 (3).

[84] M S Kenney, *'The role of national government in the restraint of global economic crime'* (1999) 7(2) J.F.C, 129, 136.

[85] E Herlin-Karnell, *'White-Collar Crime and European Financial Crisis: getting tough on EU Market Abuse'* (2012) 37(4) E. L. Rev, 481, 485.

I. Analysis of the suitability of Public Enforcement Measures

the integrity of the market is protected, those who invest on that market are also protected. Thus, while the public enforcement does not directly protect investors through allowing remedies, it should deter individuals from acting in such a way which would economically harm the investor. Thus through protecting the integrity of the capital markets, the investors are also protected. Deterrence from future offences will only be achieved if the enforcement measures are suitable[86].

a) The Criminal Offence

Edwin Sutherland defined crime as:

> *'Behaviour which is prohibited by the State as an injury to the State and against which the State may react, at least as a last resort, by punishment.'* [87]

Insider Dealing is punishable with up to seven years imprisonment and/or an unlimited fine[88], and so there is no doubt that Insider Dealing falls under this definition. However, Sutherland's use of the words 'at least as a last resort'[89] suggests that criminal sanctions should be applied fairly narrowly, and only in the right circumstances. This section analyses the criminal procedure and studies criminological theory, asking whether criminal enforcement measures are appropriate in cases of Insider Dealing.

b) Criminal Procedure: Are Juries Appropriate in Insider Dealing Trials?

Insider Dealing has been described as 'an excellent example' of the fact that the criminal law is 'wholly inappropriate' for controlling 'corporate patterns of behaviour'[90]. The complexity of the Insider Dealing offence creates difficulties for the jury system, and it has been stated that:

---

[86] Issues with the criminal regime, which degrade the deterrent effect of enforcement, are discussed below.
[87] E H Sutherland, *'White-Collar Crime'* (1949, Holt, Rinehart and Winston, Inc.), 31.
[88] Criminal Justice Act 1993 c.36, s.61.
[89] E H Sutherland, *'White-Collar Crime'* (1949, Holt, Rinehart and Winston, Inc.), 31.
[90] J Dine, *'Criminal Law in the Company Context'* (1995) Dartmouth Publishing Company Limited, 1 and 63.

> '*Lay jurors' understanding of complex and confusing evidence, the length of such trials, and the high burden of proof required to obtain a conviction have turned such trials into expensive prosecution nightmares*'. [91]

Judges have years of experience in the legal profession, whereas jurors', as laymen, are far less likely to have the standard of knowledge and experience necessary for dealing with such complex cases. Moreover, 'the accused can afford effective and astute legal representation; the offence is essentially financial, with no eyewitness testimony or visible victims to take the stand and the defendants are well-respected, established members of the community'[92]. This, plus the difficulty of understanding this complex offence and the combative nature of a criminal trial, leaves the juror vulnerable to being easily manipulated into following the most persuasive or emotive side, rather than focusing on the facts and the offence.

There has been much academic and governmental debate surrounding the suitability of trial by jury in complex Fraud cases, and Insider Dealing fits within this debate. Proposals for 'the abolition of trial by jury in complex Fraud cases' date as far back as 1986, with the Roskill Fraud Trials Committee[93]. Little action took place, however, until fairly recently, where the first steps towards Fraud trials without juries were taken with s.43 Criminal Justice Act 2003, under which prosecutors may apply to the courts for a case to be heard without a jury. Although, the decision is at the discretion of a judge and it is only in severely complex or lengthy cases that the judge will allow this application[94], this is at least a step in the right direction.

However, the past experience of this procedural issue has led to a lack in public confidence in the justice system, and it has been stated that:

---

[91] E E Avgouleas, '*The Mechanics and Regulation of Market Abuse: A Legal and Economic Analysis*' (2005, Oxford University Press), 385.

[92] E Szockyj, '*Insider Trading: The SEC Meets Carl Karcher*' ANNALS, AAPPSS, (1993) 525, 46, 46.

[93] '*Fraud Trials Committee Report*' (1986) HL Deb, 7, per Lord Elwyn-Jones at [17]: available at http://hansard.millbanksystems.com/lords/1986/feb/10/fraud-trials-committee-report (last accessed; 06/09/12).

[94] Criminal Justice Act 2003, s.43 (5).

'The public no longer believed that the legal system in England and Wales is capable of bringing the perpetrators of serious frauds expeditiously and effectively to book'. [95]

A loss of public confidence is particularly problematic; if the public have doubts about the punitive system's ability to bring justice, they are less likely to conform to the system. Thus, more needs to be done to ensure the justice achieved by the criminal courts in cases of Insider Dealing, as well as other types of complex fraud, is visible.

c) The Insider as a Criminal and Insider Dealing as a Crime; a Criminological Perspective

Another issue with the use of criminal sanctions in these circumstances surrounds the fact that Insider Dealing comes under the black letter definition of a 'white-collar crime'[96], which describes it as:

'A crime committed by a person of respectability and high social status in the course of his occupation'. [97]

The term 'white-collar' itself denotes the shirts and suits worn by professionals and business executives. In order to be found guilty of Insider Dealing, the defendant in question must be an 'insider'[98], and so must have 'inside information'[99] either through the course of his employment, profession, through simply being a member within the company, or through a contact within the company[100]. The offence is, therefore, generally committed by business executives and professionals.

White-collar crime does not conform to the general 'convention of crimes' explored in great depth by criminologists[101], and there have been arguments over whether white-collar crimes should even constitute

---

[95] *'Fraud Trials Committee Report'* (1986) HL Deb, 7, at [8]: available at http://hansard.millbanksystems.com/lords/1986/feb/10/fraud-trials-committee-report

[96] T Newburn, *'Criminolgy'* (2007, Willan Publishing), 379.

[97] E H Sutherland, *'White-Collar Crime'* (1949, Holt, Rinehart and Winston, Inc.), 9.

[98] Criminal Justice Act 1993 c.36, s.57.

[99] Ibid, s.56.

[100] See Chapter 3, below, for a more detailed discussion on the elements of the offence.

[101] E H Sutherland, *'White-Collar Crime'* (1949, Holt, Rinehart and Winston, Inc.), 3.

crimes[102]. While it has been previously suggested, in the chapter 1, that the act of Insider Dealing is serious enough to constitute a crime, this attitude poses difficulties for the effective enforcement of criminal sanctions.

Criminological studies 'have placed much emphasis' on the hypothesis that criminals are primarily a product of lower socio-economic classes of society[103]. An individual who is raised in 'poverty' and lives in 'poor housing' is associated with a 'lack of education' and 'disruptions in family life'[104]. This environment is said to encourage criminal behaviour. The social standing of a white-collar criminal creates difficulties for this general hypothesis.

Interest in white-collar crime is, however, beginning to pick up momentum in criminology. Merton's anomie/strain theory[105], for example, has been adapted by Passas to explain the deviant behavior of white-collar criminals[106]. Merton's theory argues that, when 'cultural goals'[107] are inaccessible via 'acceptable modes of achieving these goals'[108], individuals experience a strain[109]. Deviant behavior emerges as a result of this strain. Merton originally suggested that, as western culture places a lot of emphasis on materialistic goals and class separations in society create 'differentials in the accessibility' of these goals, there are some 'correlations between crime and poverty'[110].

Passas applied this theory to corporate crime, arguing that the cultural goal in this context is relative 'to necessities in the realm of business and corporations'[111]. In other words, the goal shifts from being

---

[102] E H Sutherland, *'Is "White-Collar Crime" Crime?'* (1945) 10(2) American Sociological Review, 132.

[103] E H Sutherland, *'White-Collar Crime'* (1949, Holt, Rinehart and Winston, Inc.), 6.

[104] Ibid.

[105] R K Merton, *'Social Structure and Anomie'* (1938) 3(5) American Sociological Review, 672.

[106] N Passas, *'Anomie and Corporate Deviance'* (1990) 14(2) Crime, Law and Social Change, 157.

[107] R K Merton, *'Social Structure and Anomie'* (1938) 3(5) American Sociological Review, 673.

[108] Ibid.

[109] A K Cohen, *'The Sociology of the Deviant Act: Anomie Theory and Beyond'* (1965) 30(1) American Sociological Review, 5, 6.

[110] R K Merton, *'Social Structure and Anomie'* (1938) 3(5) American Sociological Review, 680-2.

[111] N Passas, *'Anomie and Corporate Deviance'* (1990) 14(2) Crime, Law and Social Change, 157, 159.

determined by the culture of the country to being determined by the culture of the corporate world. Passas argues that corporate culture exaggerates the goals determined by society, so that merely achieving is not good enough; the business must accomplish 'never-ending achievement'[112], i.e. long-term profits. A strain is created when this goal is threatened, and this strain leads to white-collar crime.

Passas' theory of white-collar crime is limited in its application; it only applies to crimes which enhance the company's profits. Insider Dealing does not generally enhance the company's profits; it is more likely to have a detrimental effect on the company's reputation and deter further investment. It is, therefore, difficult to apply to Insider Dealing.

This lack of investigation into white-collar crime creates a clearer distinction between this type of crime and 'conventional crimes'. The laid-back public attitude towards white-collar crime that stems from this distinction and it is this that creates difficulties for the effective enforcement of criminal sanctions. The fact that Insider Dealing as a crime is not as obvious as other, more physically violent and aggressive, kinds of crime and, as explained in Chapter 1, the victims are often difficult to identify[113], desensitises the public perception of white-collar crime. The nature of this kind of crime is, thereby, 'largely impersonal'[114] and this leads to the white-collar criminal being 'freed from the stigma of crime'[115].

This creates difficulties for two of the objectives of imprisonment; retribution and deterrence[116], as the stigmas attached to a crime forms part of the deterrent effect. Stigmas can, for example, make it difficult for criminals to find or continue employment; something that is likely to be incredibly persuasive to a professional. A criminal sanction without the stigma attached to it is, thereby, less effective as a deterrent. Imprisonment is a great cost to the state and so, applying a cost-benefit analysis, it is difficult to assert that the benefit of impris-

---

[112]Ibid.

[113]E H Sutherland, *'Is "White-Collar Crime" Crime?'* (1945) 10(2) American Sociological Review, 132, 138-9.

[114]G P Gilligan, *'Regulating Against White-Collar Crime in the Financial Services Sector'* (2000) 8 (1) J.F.C, 7, 8.

[115]E H Sutherland, *'Is "White-Collar Crime" Crime?'* (1945) 10(2) American Sociological Review, 132, 138.

[116]E H Sutherland, D. R. Cressey and D. F. Luckenbill, *'Principles of Criminology'* (11th Ed. 1992, General Hall), 476.

onment outweighs the cost in cases of Insider Dealing, if the sanctions do not deter the offender effectively. This would suggest alternative enforcement measures may be necessary.

2. Regulation as Alternative Approach

It may be possible to turn to professional regulatory bodies as an alternative enforcement method. However, there is already the possibility to add disqualification orders to penalties, under s.2 Company Directors Disqualification Act 1986, and so this is already used as a deterrent. For example, in R. v. Goodman[117] the defendant was imprisoned for 18 months and disqualified from being a director for ten years. Regulation is likely to have different deterrent effects depending on the industry; a company director may still have the influence, share ownership and role within the company even if (s)he is disqualified and can no longer have the title, whereas a solicitor who is disqualified by the Solicitors Regulation Authority[118] cannot continue in their profession. Thus regulation is likely to have varying degrees of persuasiveness on professionals.

Moreover, there are possible insiders who are not under regulation, such as employees of the company; if regulation was the only method of enforcement, these potential offenders would receive no punishment. Thus, it is not plausible to suggest regulation as an alternative to public enforcement of Insider Dealing; it is, however, a useful addition.

Moreover, regulation as the only enforcement method is impractical. The European Union has been attempting to harmonise Insider Dealing laws, and as such has heavily influenced England's civil and criminal offence; the criminal offence, held under Part V Criminal Justice Act 1993, was based on the Insider Dealing Directive 1989[119] and the civil offence, held under s.118 FSMA 2000, was altered by the Financial Services and Markets Act 2000 (Market Abuse) Regulations 2005[120], after the publication of the Market Abuse Directive[121]. There has been further discussion to harmonise the European Insider Dealing

---

[117][1992] B.C.C. 625.

[118]http://www.sra.org.uk/solicitors/handbook/discproc/content.page (last accessed; 20/09/12).

[119]The Council of the European Communities, Coordinating Regulations on Insider Dealing, 1989, Directive 89/592/EEC: available at http://www.esma.europa.eu/system/files/Dir_89_592.PDF (last accessed; 07/09/12).

[120]SI 2005/381.

[121]The European Parliament and the Council of the European Union, Directive on Insider Dealing and Market Manipulation (Market Abuse) 2003, Directive

and Market Abuse regimes with the, not yet implemented, 'directive on criminal sanctions for Insider Dealing and Market Manipulation'[122]. The extent of involvement from the European Union, as well as the determination to get 'tougher on Insider Dealing'[123], 'to improve deterrence and market integrity'[124], gives the criminal and civil offences a concrete setting for as long as the UK remains a Member State.

II. Identifying Specific Enforcement Issues

The previous chapter analysed the suitability of public enforcement. However, having suitable procedures in place is futile if they are not implemented effectively. It has been stated that:

> 'The success or failure of the new [Insider Dealing] regime very much depends on the efficiency, competence, and effectiveness with which the FSA undertakes its duties and discharges its responsibilities for the benefit of UK investors and the preservation of the efficient function of the country's financial markets in today's increasingly competitive and globalised market landscape'. [125]

This chapter will analyse issues the FSA may face in attempting to 'undertake its duties and discharge its responsibilities'[126]; looking specifically at the FSA's powers of investigation and difficulty of identifying acts of Insider Dealing, and difficulties of proving the offence.

1. Problem of Identification

The FSA has fairly extensive investigatory powers; under s.166 and 167 FSMA 2000, the FSA may require specified information or doc-

---

2003/6/EC: available at http://eur-lex.europa.eu/LexUriServ/LexUriServ.do?uri=OJ:L:2003:096:0016:0016:en:PDF (last accessed; 07/09/12).
[122] http://europa.eu/rapid/pressReleasesAction.do?reference=IP/11/1218\&format=HTML\&aged=0\&language=EN\&guiLanguage=en (last accessed; 07/09/12).
[123] Ibid.
[124] Ibid.
[125] E E Avgouleas, 'The Mechanics and Regulation of Market Abuse: A Legal and Economic Analysis' (2005, Oxford University Press), 388.
[126] Ibid.

C. Public Enforcement

uments[127] and, under s.168 (3), the FSA may appoint 'one or more competent persons to conduct an investigation on its behalf'[128]. The strength in their power comes from s.177 FSMA 2000, which treats a failure to comply with a request from the FSA as contempt, making it a criminal offence[129]. This allows the FSA to extract 'self-incriminating' evidence from potential offenders[130], and thus goes some way to helping uncover acts of Insider Dealing[131].

Acts of Insider Dealing are, however, very difficult to identify; on average there are billions of pounds worth of share transaction which are traded on a daily basis on the London Stock Exchange[132], and it is not possible to investigate each transaction to ensure it was not based unfairly on inside information. Thus, the FSA have to look to 'indicators of Insider Dealing', such as 'abnormal price movements', but these 'can be easy to misinterpret'[133]. This huge task of identification is made increasingly difficult through the need to distinguish between insider's trades based on the use of inside information and insider's trades based on an accurate assessment of the market[134]; the former is illegal, whereas the latter is not. This means that a large number of Insider Deals are left unnoticed and unenforced. This large number of unnoticed offences is known as 'the Dark Figure'[135].

---

[127] Financial Services and Markets Act 2000 c. 8, s.165 and 166.
[128] Ibid, s.168 (3).
[129] Financial Services and Markets Act 2000 c. 8, s.177; *Re an enquiry under the Company Securities (Insider Dealing) Act 1985* [1988] 2 W.L.R. 33.
[130] E E Avgouleas, *'The Mechanics and Regulation of Market Abuse: A Legal and Economic Analysis'* (2005, Oxford University Press), 383.
[131] Despite the difficulty in identifying the crime, the investigatory powers of the FSA may add to the deterrent effect of enforcement, as it is likely to dissuade potential investors; this is especially relevant 'in the case of large financial institutions that rely on their reputation for doing business with investors'; E E Avgouleas, *'The Mechanics and Regulation of Market Abuse: A Legal and Economic Analysis'* (2005, Oxford University Press), 371.
[132] http://www.efinancialnews.com/story/2010-09-29/lse-trading-update-uk (last accessed; 08/09/12).
[133] http://www.fsa.gov.uk/pubs/annual/ar09_10/Section\%202.pdf (last accessed; 09/09/12).
[134] This often leaves the work of 'market makers or dealers who become aware through their work of unpublished price-sensitive 'market information' (typically relating to major acquisitions or disposals of securities) may be left in a more uncertain position'; S Griffin, *'Company Law: Fundamental Principles'* (3rd Ed. 2000, Pearson Education Limited), 185.
[135] C Stanley, *'Speculators; an interim analysis on the Blue Arrow Affair'* (1990) 9(6) Int. Bank. L, 345, 347.

It was estimated that, in 2010, 'almost a third of the takeovers on the London Stock Exchange... were preceded by suspicious share price movements, suggesting Insider Dealing or other Market Abuse may have been taking place'[136], yet the FSA received only '753 Misuse of Information notifications'[137], and there were only 11 prosecutions between 2009 and 2011[138]. It is possible that this low rate of enforcement is due to the difficulty of identifying acts of Insider Dealing. Clearly this is quite a large enforcement issue.

Despite this difficulty, the FSA seem determined to crack down on Insider Dealing; a further eleven prosecutions are set for 2012, if successful these will double the number of convictions there has currently been under the FSA's hand[139], and the majority of prosecutions brought by the FSA have been successful[140].

2. The Problem of Proof

If the FSA finds evidence of Insider Dealing in the investigation stage, they will normally commence civil or criminal proceedings, but proving these offences presents further difficulties[141]. This sub-section asks the question: is the offence of Insider Dealing too difficult for the prosecution to prove? There is a very fine line between an offence being defined too narrowly, causing problems for the prosecution, and being either unclear or too widely applicable; if the definition of the offence falls under the former, it will be difficult for the FSA to effectively enforce.

The complexity of capital market transactions and the actions of insiders adds further difficulty to defining an offence of Insider Dealing that: (a) is clearly defined without being too narrow; (b) only applies criminal sanctions to those offences which are serious enough to be criminalised; and (c) is complete, so that offenders who's actions are not serious enough to be criminalised do not go unpunished. The English

---

[136] D Prosser, *'Insider Dealing suspicions in a third of all deals'* June 2010, The Independent, (London, 11 June 2010), 40, 40.

[137] FOI2540: Request for information response, see appendix 1.

[138] http://www.fsa.gov.uk/library/communication/pr/2012/060.shtml (last accessed; 09/09/12).

[139] Ibid.

[140] Only five prosecutions brought by the FSA have been unsuccessful; FOI2540: Request for information response, see appendix 1.

[141] As outlined in the introduction, the FSA is also able to apply to the court, on behalf of the investor, for an injunction or order restitution orders also. This is discussed in further detail in the next section.

Insider Dealing regime aims to achieve this through the complementary nature of the criminal and civil offences; while the criminal offence is applied to serious, large-scale acts of Insider Dealing, the FSA is able to apply the civil regime to insiders who commit the offence on a lower scale.

This seems to work fairly well; the criminal offence is far more difficult to prove than the civil offence. Firstly, the burden of proof in criminal law is beyond reasonable doubt, whereas the civil law burden of proof is a balance of probabilities, and so the burden of proof is much higher in criminal law. In other words the prosecution, in a criminal case, must persuade the jury that there is no possible way the defendant could be innocent. This stems from the criminal law concept of innocent until proven guilty; the jury must presume the defendant is innocent until the prosecution has proven otherwise[142].

It is, therefore, more difficult to prove the individual elements of the criminal offence of Insider Dealing to the sufficient standard, than it is with the civil offence; specifically the mens rea element which involves proving that the defendant knew it was inside information from an inside source[143]. Bowen L.J. stated in *Angus v. Clifford* that 'there is no such thing as an absolute criterion which gives you a certain index to a man's mind'[144]. The difficulty of proving the criminal offence leaves it quite narrow in its application, but when complimented with the civil offence, this is not necessarily a downfall.

The fact that the standard of proof is much lower under civil law, means the civil offence is slightly easier to prove, and is thereby more widely applicable. The civil offence is also given a degree of flexibility through the use of the FSA's Handbook, which is used as authoritative guidance for the offence[145]. This handbook allows the FSA, as regulator, to define and adapt specific elements of the civil offence. In this sense, the criminal and civil offence works as a team, and one would not be effective without the other; the difficulty of proof present in the

---

[142] Although this is an ideology based on the assumption that jurors' initially keep a neutral outlook on the case. It is in fact difficult for a juror to be this neutral; naturally jurors' are judgmental and this is largely why defendant lawyers will ensure the defendant is smartly presented.

[143] Criminal Justice Act 1993 c.35, s.57(1)(a) and (b).

[144] *Angus v. Clifford* [1891] 2 Ch. 449, per Bowen L.J, at [471].

[145] Financial Services and Markets Act 2000 c.8, ss.119-122; Financial Services Authority Handbook, *Code of Market Conduct (MAR 1)*, available at http://fsahandbook.info/FSA/html/handbook/MAR/1 (last accessed; 20/09/12)

criminal offence ensures it is confined to the more serious cases, while the wider application of the civil regime ensures contraventions of the offence do not go unpunished.

3. Civil Remedies and Public Enforcement

Under s.383 FSMA 2000, the FSA may apply to the court requesting a restitution order, and the court will award this if it is satisfied that (a) the defendant is guilty of the offence[146] and (b) the defendant made a profit or the investor suffered a loss as a result[147]. The general principle[148] of the law of restitution is that it reverses a situation where party A has been 'unjustly enriched'[149] at the expense of party B[150]. This would have the advantage of directly remedying the investor; civil penalties are a punitive measure and so are unable to do this. It would, therefore, go further to remedying the investor.

However, the FSA have expressed a reluctance to exercise this power; stating 'we are not convinced that it would be appropriate for the FSA to exercise its civil enforcement powers for the benefit of [victims of Insider Dealing]. It is not clear to us that their interests can be said to have been prejudiced to such an extent as would warrant action by the FSA to secure redress on their behalf'[151]. This attitude towards awarding restitutionary damages, plus the fact that this remedy is reliant on the FSA's investigations and detection of Insider Dealing, which, as highlighted above, often leave violations of the offence uncovered, may lead to many investors out of pocket. For this reason private enforcement of civil remedies is also necessary; the availability of which is discussed in section II, below.

---

[146] Financial Services and Markets Act 2000 c.8, s. 323 (1).

[147] Ibid, s. 323 (2) (a) and (b).

[148] Restitution is also available in cases of civil wrongs. This is, however, considered as a distinctly different claim from restitution for unjust enrichment (*Sempra Metals Ltd (formerly Metallgesellschaft Ltd) v. Inland Revenue Commissioners and Another* [2008] 1 A.C. 561, per Lord Mance, at [649]) and, as Insider Dealing results in the insider gaining at the expense of the investor, a claim for restitution on the basis of unjust enrichment is applicable. Thus, this dissertation does not explore restitution for civil wrongs.

[149] The nature of a claim for unjust enrichment is described in more detail in chapter 5.

[150] W V H Rogers, *'Tort'* (17th Ed. 2006,Sweet & Maxwell Limited), 13.

[151] Financial Services Authority, *'Financial services regulation: Enforcing the new regime'* (1989) Consultation Paper 17,, 58-9. Available at: http://www.fsa.gov.uk/pubs/cp/cp17.pdf (last accessed; 16/09/12).

III. Summarising Arguments for Section I: Public Enforcement

Chapter 2 established that the issues present in public enforcement of Insider Dealing are largely due to the public perception of white-collar crime and the criminal procedure. It has been stated that:

> '*Where the task of education has been grappled with effectively, the goal of enforcement is made somewhat simpler*'.[152]

The enforcement record has been used by academics to argue that 'criminal law is often an inappropriate way to regulate and deter financial market abuse'[153]. However, this situation has been improved slightly since the introduction of the civil offence, as this acts to compliment the criminal provisions; the civil regime is easier to prove and so is useful where criminal punishment would be too heavy. Criminal sanctions should only be implemented where there has been a serious violation of the relevant legal provisions[154], and so the criminal law cannot be the sole method of enforcement. Despite the difficulties in identifying Insider Dealing, the FSA seem determined to crack down on this offence, and with this determination and the complementary nature of the civil and criminal offence, public enforcement measures seem to work effectively. Moreover, investigative measures themselves can add to the deterrent effect of enforcement. It should not be forgotten, however, that the issues surrounding the public perception of white-collar crime and the issues surrounding the public enforcement of civil remedies are still very much prevalent, and these should be resolved. A possibility for the resolution of the issues surrounding public enforcement of civil remedies would be to allow private enforcement of Insider Dealing and it is this which will now be analysed.

---

[152] M S Kenney, '*The role of national government in the restraint of global economic crime*' (1999) 7(2) J.F.C, 129, 134.

[153] E E Avgouleas, '*The Mechanics and Regulation of Market Abuse: A Legal and Economic Analysis*' (2005, Oxford University Press), 324.

[154] J Eeklaar and J Bell, '*Oxford Essays in Jurisprudence*' (3rd Series, 1987, Oxford University Press); A. Ashworth, '*Belief, Intent and Criminal Liability*', 1.

D. Private Enforcement

It was stated in chapter 3 that an investor, who has suffered a loss as a result of Insider Dealing, should be able to bring a private action under English law. This is, however, incredibly difficult, as it is generally thought that allowing a private right of action would reduce the certainty that English law provides corporate transactions. Callum McCarthy, then chairman of the FSA, stated in 2004:

> 'the great majority of our enforcement cases have, until now, been resolved through the administrative process... I continue to hope that we can maintain confidence in... [this] process and promote efficient, orderly and clean markets without a dramatic increase in the number of cases referred to the Tribunal. It is in all our interests – not simply the FSA's – that this should happen. The UK has traditionally enjoyed over North America the advantage of being a less litigious society. There is much to be lost if that advantage is eroded'. [155]

This section analyses where it is possible for an investor to bring a private action, looking at actions for both civil and equitable remedies[156].

---

[155] C McCarthy, 'Mansion House Speech' 21 September 2004 FSA. Available at: http://www.fsa.gov.uk/library/communication/speeches/2004/sp195.shtml (last accessed 17/09/12).

[156] Under s.63 (2) Criminal Justice Act 1993 c.36, prosecution of Insider Dealing does not render the contract 'void or unenforceable' and, under s.131 Financial Services and Markets Act 2000 c.8, the imposition of a penalty 'does not make any transaction void or unenforceable'. Thus actions under contract law are not applicable here.

D. *Private Enforcement*

I. Civil Remedies and Private Enforcement

This chapter explores the rights of action available to investors to recover damages. It will analyse whether there is right of action arising directly out of the relevant Insider Dealing provisions held under FSMA 2000, and then to move on to discuss the alternative options under English tort law.

1. Implied rights of action Arising out of Insider Dealing provisions

Under s.150 FSMA 2000, private persons may have a right of action against an authorised person, if that authorised person contravenes a provision of the FSMA 2000 and the individual suffers a loss as a result. Thus it would seem that individuals may have a private right of action in cases of Insider Dealing. The Financial Services and Markets Act 2000 (Rights of Action) Regulations 2001[157], suggest that the right of action stipulated under s.150 FSMA 2000 applies in cases of Insider Dealing; under regulation 6 (3) (b) of this legislation[158], the private right of action under s.150 FSMA 2000 applies where:

> '*The rule that has been contravened is directed at ensuring that transactions in any security or contractually based investment... are not effected with the benefit of unpublished information that, if made public, would be likely to affect the price of that security or investment*'. [159]

Assuming this regulation applies, Insider Dealing would be actionable even 'at the suit of a person who is not a private person'[160]. This would create a widely applicable right of action, available to both private and institutional investors.

However, it is questionable whether the s.150 FSMA 2000 right applies to acts of Insider Dealing; under s.150 (2) exclusions to this right of action may arise[161] and, under the FSA's Code of Market Conduct

---

[157] SI 2001/2256.
[158] Ibid, reg. 6 (3) (b).
[159] Ibid.
[160] Ibid, regulation 6 (2).
[161] Financial Services and Markets Act 2000 c.8, s.150 (2).

sch.5.2[162], there are currently no rules regarding private rights of action for cases of Market Abuse. Furthermore, contraventions which often lead to Market Abuse, such as contraventions of disclosure rules[163], are expressly excluded[164]. This suggests that private rights of action for Insider Dealing will also be excluded, particularly when viewed with the FSA's reluctance to award remedies in cases of Insider Dealing[165] and the political concerns over allowing private rights of action described above[166].

The courts have also shed doubt on the applicability of this right, recently stating in *Hall v. Cable and Wireless Plc*[167] that the relevant sections of FSMA 2000 'indicate that the intent of Parliament was that the object of the Act would be achieved by the imposition of penalties or restitution orders pursuant to ss.123 and 383. In those circumstances the absence of an express cause of action at the suit of a private person is a clear indication that none was intended'[168]. This seems to block any private right of action which could have been implied under s.118 FSMA 2000, and so an investor who has suffered as a result of Insider Dealing will have to look to alternative rights of action if (s)he wishes to pursue remedies privately.

2. Alternative Rights of Action

Considering the ambiguity surrounding private rights of action arising directly out of Insider Dealing provisions, it is necessary to expand this discussion. Thus this section examines the role of the Financial Services Ombudsman and explores rights of action under tort law as alternative rights of action.

---

[162]http://fsahandbook.info/FSA/html/handbook/MAR/Sch/5 (last accessed; 10/09/12).

[163]Financial Services and Markets Act 2000 c.8, s.73A.

[164]For the exclusion of disclosure rules specifically see: Financial Services and Markets Act 2000 c.8, s.150 (4).

[165]Explained in more detail under 'Civil Remedies and Public Enforcement', Chapter 3.

[166]C McCarthy, 'Mansion House Speech' 21 September 2004 FSA. Available at: http://www.fsa.gov.uk/library/communication/speeches/2004/sp195.shtml (last accessed17/09/12).

[167][2011] B.C.C 543.

[168]Ibid, per Teare J, at [549-550].

D. *Private Enforcement*

a) Financial Services Ombudsman[169]

An investor may have a right of action through the Financial Services Ombudsman[170], under Part XVI and sch. 17 FSMA 2000. The Financial Services Ombudsman is able to deal with complaints regarding the selling and buying of shares[171] and so may be able to handle complaints regarding Insider Dealing. This option does, however, have a number of limitations, one of which is the financial limitations of the ombudsman; (s)he can award no more than £150,000[172]. This could be marginal in large cases of Insider Dealing; the FSA have, for example, recently given Confiscation Orders amounting to over £1.5 million for profits made out of Insider Deals of nearly £600,000[173]. It could be argued that the Insider's victim has only suffered a loss of opportunity and, thus, compensation of £150,000 would go some way to remedying this loss. However, this argument ignores the importance placed on investor confidence and integrity of capital markets; awarding a small percentage of the profits made by an inside deal is not likely to act as a deterrent, nor is it likely to give the investor confidence in the markets ability to ensure fair and equal trading opportunities. Given the fact that the justifications surrounding Insider Dealing provisions revolve around the impetus to protect investors and capital markets this limitation is quite harmful.

A further limitation is the fact that the Financial Ombudsman Service is only available to those who are 'eligible'. This includes consumers, micro-enterprises and charities or trustees of trusts with an

---

[169] For claims against insolvent firms the investor should direct their complaint to the Financial Compensation Scheme (Financial Services and Markets Act 2000 c.8, Part XV): http://www.fscs.org.uk/what-we-cover/questions-and-answers/ (last accessed; 18/09/12).

[170] http://www.financial-ombudsman.org.uk/ (last accessed; 10/09/12).

[171] http://fsahandbook.info/FSA/html/handbook/DISP/2/3 (last accessed; 10/09/12); http://fsahandbook.info/FSA/glossary-html/handbook/Glossary/R?definition=G974 (last accessed; 10/09/12).

[172] http://fsahandbook.info/FSA/html/handbook/DISP/3/7 (last accessed; 10/09/12).

[173] http://www.fsa.gov.uk/library/communication/pr/2012/082.shtml (last accessed 11/09/12).

income or value of less than one million pounds[174], and so is generally not available to institutional investors or financial institutions[175].

b) Claims under Tort Law

aa) Negligent Misstatement

This claim is, again, limited in its application; in order to prove negligence there must be a duty of care and so this right of action will only arise where there is a 'special relationship' between the insider and the investor[176], which was said to apply 'where persons hold themselves out as possessing special skill and are thus under a duty to exercise it with reasonable care'[177]. In order to establish a special relationship the investor must prove:

> '(1) the advice is required for a purpose, whether particularly specified or generally described, which is made known, either actually or inferentially, to the adviser at the time when the advice is given; (2) the adviser knows, either actually or inferentially, that his advice will be communicated to the advisee, either specifically or as a member of an ascertainable class, in order that it should be used by the advisee for that purpose; (3) it is known either actually or inferentially, that the advice so communicated is likely to be acted upon by the advisee for that purpose without independent inquiry, and (4) it is so acted upon by the advisee to his detriment.' [178]

This relationship would be difficult to find between an investor and an insider, and so this right of action will only generally apply between

---

[174] http://fsahandbook.info/FSA/html/handbook/DISP/2/7 (last accessed; 10/09/12).

[175] However, institutional investors and financial institutions are the big players in capital markets. They are thereby more likely to have suffered a greater loss than a consumer if they become a victim of Insider Dealing, and so it is unlikely they would turn to the Financial Ombudsman Service for compensation, given its financial limitation. This does not, however, take away from the limited application of this option.

[176] *Hedley Byrne & Co. Ltd. Appellants; v. Heller & Partners Ltd. Respondents* [1963] 3 W.L.R. 101.

[177] Ibid per Lord Hodson, at [510].

[178] *Caparo Industries Plc. Respondents v. Dickman and Others Appellants* [1990] 2 A.C. 605, per Lord Oliver of Aylmerton, at [638].

investors and 'investment advisors and auditors'[179]. The fact that negligent misrepresentation is only actionable against those that advise investors, rather than those that sell as insiders, demeans the deterrent effect that private enforcement has, and so fails to complement the public enforcement methods.

bb) The tort of Deceit

The tort of deceit was established by *Pasley and Another v Freeman*[180], where it was stated that:

> '*It is admitted, that the action is new in point of precedent: but it is insisted that the law recognises principles on which it may be supported. The principle on which it is contended to lie is, that wherever deceit or falsehood is practised to the detriment of another, the law will give redress*'[181].

This tort has been applied to Insider Dealing in the case of *Miza Mohamet Tackey v R. S. F. McBain*,[182] where a large amount of oil had been found on the company's property. The defendant was said to have 'improperly concealed the same from the general body of the shareholders until April 19, with fraudulent intent, and... he orally denied to persons other than the plaintiff or his agent the receipt thereof, thereby deluding the public, meaning the dealers and holders of shares including the plaintiff, who in consequence were induced to sell at less than the true market value of their shares'[183]. This would suggest that where the insider has deceived the investor to his/her detriment, the law will remedy him/her under the tort of deceit. It should be noted, however, that this case precedes the FSMA 2000 and so it is questionable whether an investor will still be able to rely on this principle, or whether the court will adopt the view taken in *Hall v. Cable and Wireless Plc*,[184] described above.

It is quite difficult to prove this tort. In order to successfully bring an action in the tort of deceit, the investor must prove: (a) the representations made were fraudulent, i.e. they were false and were made with

---

[179] E.E. Avegouleas, '*The Mechanics and Regulation of Market Abuse: A Legal and Economic Analysis*' (2005, Oxford University Press), p. 421.
[180] (1789) 3 Term Reports 51.
[181] Ibid, per Grose J, at [53].
[182] [1912] A.C. 186.
[183] Ibid, at [186].
[184] [2011] B.C.C 543.

fraudulent intent, i.e. knowing they were false; and (b) these fraudulent misrepresentations were 'material' to 'produce... [in the investor's]... mind 'an erroneous belief'[185]. The investor is likely to face challenges when proving point (a). The difficulty in proving intent described in chapter 3 above is thereby also applicable here; although the standard of proof here is lower than criminal trials[186], the investor does not have the same powers of investigation as the FSA and so does not have the ability to commence an investigation into the insider's actions to the same degree.

This difficulty is added to, as the test to determine whether or not the representations made were fraudulent does not derive from the ordinary meaning of the words within the representations or even from what the reasonable man would have construed from it, but from what the insider intended them to mean[187]. The investor will therefore find it very difficult to succeed in a claim of this kind.

II. Analysing Equity's role

Equity is a 'branch of the law' said to assist the legal system 'by the introduction of a discretionary power to do justice in particular cases where the strict rules of law cause hardship'[188]. It thereby has connotations with fairness and justice and so, considering the fact that justifications for Insider Dealing provisions are primarily based on the fair and equal operations of the market, it would seem logical that equity would provide a remedy where an investor has been a victim of an insider's trade. Moreover, one of the maxims of equity states that *'Equity will not suffer a wrong to be without a remedy'* [189]; i.e. 'equity will intervene to protect a right which, perhaps because of some technical defect, is not enforceable at law'[190]. Thus the injustice presented by acts of Insider Dealing and the difficulties the investor may face bring-

---

[185] *William Smith v David Chadwick, John Oldfield Chadwick, Ebenezer Adamson, and Edwin Collier* (1883-84) L.R. 9 App. Cas. 187, per Earl of Selborne L.C, at [190].

[186] The civil standard of proof applies; beyond reasonable doubt.

[187] *Baron Uno Carl Samuel Akerhielm and Another Appellants; v Rolf De Mare and Others Respondents* [1959] 3 W.L.R. 108.

[188] J E Martin, *'Modern Equity'* (18th Ed. 2008, Sweet & Maxwell), 3-4.

[189] Ibid, p. 30.

[190] Ibid.

ing a private claim under civil law suggest that equity should provide the investor with a right of action here.

However, this is an oversimplified approach; equitable principles are far more complex than this and are by no means 'synonymous with justice'[191], as this rather broad statement would suggest. The discretionary nature of equitable remedies leaves them only available in very specific circumstances. This chapter analyses equity as a method of private enforcement in Insider Dealing cases.

1. Breach of Fiduciary duties

Fiduciaries are not entitled to make a profit from their position[192], and so if it can be found that a fiduciary relationship exists in a case of Insider Dealing, the investor may be able to apply to the courts for an equitable remedy, such as accounting for profits or equitable compensation, on the basis of the fiduciary's breach of duty.

The existence of a fiduciary relationship will, however, be difficult for the investor to establish. The nature of a fiduciary relationship involves one party acting 'on behalf of another in a particular matter in circumstances which give rise to a relationship of trust and confidence'[193]. The courts in *Loyds Bank Ltd v Bundy*[194] stated that the 'elements necessary to establish the existence of the special fiduciary relationship' are '(1) advice given; (2) reliance upon that advice; (3) an element of confidentiality; (4) the person in whom the confidence is imposed has some interest in the transaction so that there is a conflict of interest; (5) the knowledge of the reliance upon the advice'[195].

Insider Dealing generally involves voluntary transactions between two individual parties, and so the very specific definition of this relationship makes it difficult for victims of Insider Dealing to rely on. It may, however, apply where the inside information 'has been entrusted in confidence to the broker or investment adviser' or in the case of directors[196]. Even in the instance of directors, however, the fiduciary duty

---

[191] Ibid, p. 3.

[192] *George Bray v. John Rawlinson Ford* [1896] A.C. 44, per Lord Herschell, at [51].

[193] *Bristol and West Building Society v. Mothew* [1998] Ch. 1, per Millet J, at [18].

[194] [1975] Q.B. 326.

[195] Ibid, per Cairns LJ, at [332].

[196] E E Avgouleas, *'The Mechanics and Regulation of Market Abuse: A Legal and Economic Analysis'* (2005, Oxford University Press), 430.

II. Analysing Equity's role

is likely to be owed to the company, and not the investor[197]; 'modern-day investors usually effect their trades on anonymous markets. Thus, it is rather unlikely that any pre-existing fiduciary relationship can be identified between injured investors and'[198] insiders. Although this has a deterrent effect in punishing the insider, by requiring him/her to compensate the company[199], it does little to compensate the investor.

2. Unjust Enrichment and Restitution

The FSA's power to award the remedy of restitution in Insider Dealing cases, described above, does not affect an investor's right to bring a private action for restitution[200]. Thus an investor, who has fallen victim of an insider's deal, will be able to bring a private claim for restitution providing the court is satisfied that: (a) the insider was enriched; (b) at the expense of the investor; and (c) the enrichment was unjust[201].

The law takes a fairly strict view with regard to what is considered to be unjust, in an attempt to ensure 'it is not an invitation for an exercise of idiosyncratic discretion to remedy unfairness nor... an immediate panacea to difficult issues in private law'[202]. It has, however, been accepted that 'equitable fraud' can be considered a ground for restitution. This can be 'presumed or inferred from the circumstances or conditions of the parties contracting: weakness on one side, usury on the other, or extortion or advantage taken of that weakness'[203]. There are three elements under this ground: (1) 'one party has been at a serious disadvantage to the other... so that circumstances existed of which unfair advantage could be taken'; (2) 'this weakness of the one party... [was] exploited by the other in some morally culpable manner'; and (3) 'the resulting transaction has been, not merely hard or

---

[197] Companies Act 2006 c.46, s.170

[198] E E Avgouleas, *'The Mechanics and Regulation of Market Abuse: A Legal and Economic Analysis'* (2005, Oxford University Press), 436.

[199] *Regal (Hastings) Ltd v. Gulliver and Others* [1967] 2 A.C. 134; *Boardman and Another Appellants v. Phipps Respondent* [1966] 3 W.L.R. 1009.

[200] Financial Services and Markets Act 2000 c.8, s.383 (9).

[201] *Banque Financière de ka Cité v Parc (Battersea) Ltd and others* [1998] 1 All ER 737, per Lord Steyn, at [740].

[202] S Degeling and J Edelman, *'Unjust Enrichment in Commercial Law'* (2008, Thomson Reuters (Professional) Australia Pty Limited t/a Lawbook Co.), 4.

[203] *Earl of Chesterfield and Others Executors of John Spencer v. Sir Abraham Janssen* (1751) 28 E.R. 82, per Lord Hardwicke, at [101].

D. Private Enforcement

improvident, but overreaching and oppressive'[204]. It was stated in *Alec Lobb Garages Ltd v Total Oil Great Britain Ltd*[205] that 'where there has been a sale at an undervalue, the under-value has almost always been substantial, so that it calls for an explanation, and is in itself indicative of the presence of some fraud, undue influence, or other such feature'[206]. This suggests that an investor would be able to bring a claim for Insider Dealing under this principle.

The nature of securities as assets may, however, make it difficult for an investor to succeed in a claim for restitution, as the property will be hard to trace. Tracing is the 'means of getting to particular remedies'.[207] It is effectively the process of tracking the misappropriated property in question, and so the asset must be able to be 'identifiable'[208]. 'The exercise of tracing allows one asset to stand in the place of another'[209], thus this is particularly relevant to cases of Insider Dealing, as 'a substitute [i.e. the purchase money,] stands, in the place of'[210] the original asset, i.e. the securities. The difficulty here is that the securities are transformed into money and then this money is likely to be mixed with other proceeds; 'in such a case the legal title on the asset is lost'[211].

This is, however, the view of common law tracing, under equity tracing is slightly different, as equitable tracing is based on the concept of trust.[212] In other words, the claimant is said to be the beneficial owner of the property and the defendant the trustee.[213] It is thereby necessary for an investor, who wishes to pursue tracing under equity, to establish a fiduciary relationship; as highlighted above, this presents difficulties for the investor.

---

[204] *Alec Lobb (Garages) Ltd. and Others v. Total Oil Great Britain Ltd.* [1983] 1 W.L.R. 87, per Peter Millett Q.C., at [94-95].
[205] [1983] 1 W.L.R. 87.
[206] Ibid, per Peter Millett Q.C., at [95].
[207] A Burrows, *'The Law of Restitution'* (3rd Ed. 2011 Oxford University Press), 117
[208] *Agip (Africa) Ltd. v. Jackson and Others* [1990] Ch. 265, per Millett J, at [285].
[209] L D Smith, *'The Law of Tracing'* (1997, Oxford University Press), 17.
[210] Ibid, 6.
[211] E E Avgouleas, *'The Mechanics and Regulation of Market Abuse: A Legal and Economic Analysis'* (2005, Oxford University Press), 437.
[212] Ibid.
[213] *Attorney-General for Hong Kong Appellants v. Charles Warwick Reid and Others Respondents* [1994] 1 AC 324, per Lord Templeman, at [330].

3. Summarising Arguments for section II: Private enforcement

This section has suggested that the civil rights of action are ambiguous, unclear and limited in their application, and the nature of the fiduciary relationship makes it incredibly difficult for an investor to successfully bring a claim under equity. Rider stated that:

> 'In English law... in the vast majority of market transactions it is very unlikely that a duty will arise between the insider and his casual counterparty so as to afford that person any realistic opportunity at law for compensation let alone recission... There is a marked reluctance in the judiciary to contemplate affording civil claims to investors, particularly those in the market'.[214]

It seems that there is much truth in this statement; it is incredibly difficult for an investor to bring a private action where (s)he is a victim of an insider's deal and, considering the EU's priority in protection of the investor, it is submitted that this stance should be rethought.

III. Concluding Thoughts and Possible suggestions for Reform; what can be proposed from the Above Arguments?

The EU has shifted the aim of Insider Dealing provisions from a 'company law approach', based on the fiduciary relationship and protection of the company, to a 'securities markets approach', based on protection of the capital markets and investors[215]. This dissertation has argued that the current English law on this matter does not sufficiently achieve this aim. Avegouleas stated that:

---

[214] B A K Rider and M Andenas, *'Developments in European Company Law'* (1997 Kluwer Law International Ltd.), 22

[215] P L Davies, 'The European Community's Directive on Insider Dealing: From Company Law to Securities Markets Regulation' [1991] Oxford J. Legal Stud. 92, 92.

D. Private Enforcement

> 'Essentially, [the English law on Insider Dealing]... shelters financial institutions and other persons from the consequences of their own actions'.[216]

There is a certain degree of truth in this statement; the FSA's reluctance to apply for restitutionary damages on behalf of the investor[217] and the difficulties an investor would face in bringing a private action for Insider Dealing make it incredibly difficult for an investor to claim damages for any loss they may have suffered. In this sense, an insider who trades on the basis of unfair information is not required to remedy the investor who suffered as a result. Moreover, the public perception of the white-collar criminal has the effect of decreasing the deterrent effect of the sanctions and the issues surrounding the use of juries in complex cases, such as Insider Dealing, has diminished the public confidence in the punitive system's ability to bring justice. The fact that an insider as a criminal is not stigmatised and (s)he is not liable to pay the investor remedies weakens the protection the law offers an investor.

The current legislation primarily aims to protect investors through public enforcement, i.e. using the civil and criminal measures as a deterrent. This is strange considering the Fair Play approach taken as part of the justification for Insider Dealing provisions; this theory generally 'gives rise to a theory of compensation or restitution, but not punishment'[218]. Academics view this as one of the key weaknesses of this theory, and so the fact that Insider Dealing has broken this pattern suggests the law would be fairly strong. However, due to the issues surrounding the public perception and detection of contraventions of Insider Dealing provisions, this is not particularly successful. Tackling these issues is an incredibly daunting task; to have such a wide public influence would be incredibly difficult and the fact that this public attitude has well grounded for quite some time, particularly the attitude to white-collar crime, makes this task even harder. Moreover, the issues surrounding detection are due to the nature of the offence; altering this while ensuring Insider Dealing is still prohibited, rather than regulated,

---

[216] E E Avegouleas, *'The Mechanics and Regulation of Market Abuse: A Legal and Economic Analysis'* (2005, Oxford University Press), 395.

[217] Financial Services Authority, *'Financial services regulation: Enforcing the new regime'* (1989) Consultation Paper 17, p.58-59. Available at: http://www.fsa.gov.uk/pubs/cp/cp17.pdf (last accessed; 16/09/12).

[218] M Matravers, *'Justice and Punishment: The rationale of Coercion'* (2003, Oxford Scholarship Online), 58.

III. Concluding Thoughts and Possible suggestions for Reform; what can be proposed from the Above Arguments?

will be very difficult, and regulation is not sufficient as a standalone alternative to public enforcement.

Issues surrounding the enforcement of private remedies are, in comparison, far easier to rectify and it is submitted that these issues should be addressed in order for the English law on Insider Dealing to sufficiently protect investors; this is the main proposal of this dissertation. The simplest way to ensure investors have a private right of action would be to imply one under s.118 FSMA 2000; this would also ensure that the right of action would be far reaching as, under the assumptions based on the Financial Services and Markets Act 2000 (Rights of Action) Regulations 2001,[219] private rights of action would be available to both private and institutional investors[220]. This would also diffuse the confusion surrounding the applicability of alternative civil private rights of action and equitable principles.

---

[219] SI 2001/2256.
[220] Ibid regulation, 6 (2).

E. Reference List

I. List of Cases

Agip (Africa) Ltd. v. Jackson and Others [1990] Ch. 265.

Alex Lobb (Garages) Ltd. and Others v. Total Oil Great Britain Ltd. [1983] 1 W.L.R. 87.

Angus v. Clifford [1891] 2 Ch. 449.

Attorney-General for Hong Kong Appellants v. Charles Warwick Reid and Others Respondents [1994] 1 AC 324.

Banque Financière de ka Cité v Parc (Battersea) Ltd and others [1998] 1 All ER 737.

Baron Uno Carl Samuel Akerhielm and Another Appellants; v Rolf De Mare and Others Respondents [1959] 3 W.L.R. 108.

Boardman and Another Appellants v. Phipps Respondent [1966] 3 W.L.R. 1009.

Bristol and West Building Society v. Mothew [1998] Ch. 1.

Caparo Industries Plc. Respondents v. Dickman and Others Appellants [1990] 2 A.C. 605.

Earl of Chesterfield and Others Executors of John Spencer v. Sir Abraham Janssen (1751) 28 E.R. 82.

E. Reference List

George Bray v. John Rawlinson Ford [1896] A.C. 44.

Hall v. Cable and Wireless Plc [2011] B.C.C 543.

Hedley Byrne & Co. Ltd. Appellants; v. Heller & Partners Ltd. Respondents [1963] 3 W.L.R. 101.

Loyds Bank Ltd v Bundy [1975] Q.B. 326.

Miza Mohamet Tackey v R. S. F. McBain [1912] A.C. 186.

Pasley and Another v Freeman (1789) 3 Term Reports 51.

Percival v. Wright [1902] 2 Ch. 421.

R v. Christopher McQuoid [2010] 1 Cr. App.R. (S.) 43.

R. v. Goodman [1992] B.C.C. 625.

Re an enquiry under the Company Securities (Insider Dealing) Act 1985 [1988] 2 W.L.R. 33.

Regal (Hastings) Ltd v. Gulliver and Others [1967] 2 A.C. 134.

Sempra Metals Ltd (formerly Metallgesellschaft Ltd) v. Inland Revenue Commissioners and Another [2008] 1 A.C. 561.

William Derry, J. C. Wakefield, M. M. Moore, J. Pethick, and S. J. Wilde v Sir Henry William Peek, Baronet (1889) L.R. 14 App. Cas. 337.

William Smith v David Chadwick, John Oldfield Chadwick, Ebenezer Adamson, and Edwin Collier (1883-84) L.R. 9 App. Cas. 187.

II. List of Statutes

Companies Act 1980 c.22.

Company Securities (Insider Dealing) Act 1985 c.8.

Company Directors Disqualification Act 1986 c.46.

The Council of the European Communities, Coordinating Regulations on Insider Dealing, 1989, Directive 89/592/EEC: available at http://www.esma.europa.eu/system/files/Dir_89_592.PDF (last accessed; 07/09/12).

Criminal Justice Act 1993 c.36.

Financial Services and Markets Act 2000 c.8.

Financial Services and Markets Act 2000 (Rights of Action) Regulations 2001 SI 2001/2256.

Criminal Justice Act 2003 c.44.

The European Parliament and the Council of the European Union, Directive on Insider Dealing and Market Manipulation (Market Abuse) 2003, Directive 2003/6/EC: available at http://eur-lex.europa.eu/LexUriServ/LexUriServ.do?uri=OJ:L:2003:096:0016:0016:en:PDF (last accessed; 07/09/12).

Financial Services and Markets Act 2000 (Market Abuse) Regulations 2005 SI 2005/381.

Companies Act 2006 c.46.

III. Bibliography of Reference Sources

A. Burrows, *'The Law of Restitution'* (3rd Ed. 2011 Oxford University Press).

A. H. Shand, *'Free Market Morality: The Political economy of the Austrian School'* (1990 Routledge).

A. Hudson, *'The Law of Finance'* (2009, Thomson Reuters (Legal) Limited).

A. F. Loke, *'From the fiduciary theory to information abuse: the changing fabric of Insider Trading law in the U.K., Australia and Singapore'* (2006) 54(1) The American Journal of Comparative Law, 123.

A. K. Cohen, *'The Sociology of the Deviant Act: Anomie Theory and Beyond'* (1965) 30(1) American Sociological Review, 5.

A. Shleifer, *'Inefficient Markets: an Introduction to Behavioural Finance'* (2000, Oxford University Press).

Agip (Africa) Ltd. v. Jackson and Others [1990] Ch. 265.

Alex Lobb (Garages) Ltd. and Others v. Total Oil Great Britain Ltd. [1983] 1 W.L.R. 87.

Angus v. Clifford [1891] 2 Ch. 449.

Attorney-General for Hong Kong Appellants v. Charles Warwick Reid and Others Respondents [1994] 1 AC 324.

B. A. K. Rider and M. Andenas, *'Developments in European Company Law'* (1997 Kluwer Law International Ltd.).

B. R. Cheffins, *'Does the Law Matter? The Separation of Ownership and Control in the United Kingdom'* (2001) 30 J. Legal. Stud, 459.

Banque Financière de ka Cité v Parc (Battersea) Ltd and others [1998] 1 All ER 737.

Baron Uno Carl Samuel Akerhielm and Another Appellants; v Rolf De Mare and Others Respondents [1959] 3 W.L.R. 108.

Boardman and Another Appellants v. Phipps Respondent [1966] 3 W.L.R. 1009.

Bristol and West Building Society v. Mothew [1998] Ch. 1.

C. McCarthy, 'Mansion House Speech' 21 September 2004 FSA. Available at: http://www.fsa.gov.uk/library/communication/speeches/2004/sp195.shtml (last accessed 17/09/12).

C. Stanley, *'Speculators; an interim analysis on the Blue Arrow Affair'* (1990) 9(6) Int. Bank. L, 345.

Caparo Industries Plc. Respondents v. Dickman and Others Appellants [1990] 2 A.C. 605.

Companies Act 1980 c.22.

Companies Act 2006 c.46.

Company Directors Disqualification Act 1986 c.46.

Company Securities (Insider Dealing) Act 1985 c.8.

Criminal Justice Act 1993 c.36.

Criminal Justice Act 2003 c.44.

D. Ormerod, *'The Fraud Act - Criminalising Lying?'* [2007] Crim. L.R., 193.

D. Prosser, 'Insider Dealing Suspicions in a Third of All Deals, says Regulator' *The Independent* (London, 11 June 2010).

D. W. Carlton and D. R. Fischel, *'The Regulation of Insider Trading'* (1993) 35(5) Stanford Law Review, 857.

E. E. Avegouleas, *'The Mechanics and Regulation of Market Abuse: A Legal and Economic Analysis'* (2005, Oxford University Press).

E. F. Fama, *'Efficient Capital Markets: a Review of Theory and Empirical Work'* (1970) 25(2) Journal of Finance, 383.

E. F. Fama, *'Efficient Capital Markets: II'* (1991) 46(5) Journal of Finance, 1575.

E. H. Sutherland, D. R. Cressey and D. F. Luckenbill, *'Principles of Criminology'* (11th Ed. 1992, General Hall).

E. H. Sutherland, *'Is "White-Collar Crime" Crime?'* (1945) 10(2) American Sociological Review, 132.

E. H. Sutherland, *'White Collar Crime'* (1949, Holt, Rinehart and Winston, Inc.).

E. Herlin-Karnell, *'White-Collar Crime and European Financial Crisis: getting tough on EU Market Abuse'* (2012) 37(4) E.L. Rev, 481.

E. Szockyj, *'Insider Trading: The SEC Meets Carl Karcher'* ANNALS, AAPPSS, (1993) 525, 46.

Earl of Chesterfield and Others Executors of John Spencer v. Sir Abraham Janssen (1751) 28 E.R. 82.

F. Allen and R. Herring, *'Banking Regulation versus Securities Market Regulation'* (2001) The Wharton Financial Institutions Center Working Paper, University of Pensylvania, 1.

F. H. Easterbrook, *'Insider Trading, Secret Agents, Evidentiary Privileges and the Production of Information'* [1981] Supt. Ct. Rev, 309.

F. Song and A. Thakor, *'Banks and Capital Markets as a Coevolving Financial System'* [2010] Vox: http://www.voxeu.org/article/banks-and-capital-markets-coevolving-financial-system (last accessed; 20/08/12).

F. Song and A. V. Thakor, *'Financial System Architecture and the Co-Evolution of Banks and Capital Markets'* (2010) 120(547), 1021.

Financial Services and Markets Act 2000 c.8.

Financial Services and Markets Act 2000 (Market Abuse) Regulations 2005 SI 2005/381.

Financial Services and Markets Act 2000 (Rights of Action) Regulations 2001 SI 2001/2256.

Financial Services Authority, *'Financial services regulation: Enforcing the new regime'* (1989) Consultation Paper 17. Available at: http://www.fsa.gov.uk/pubs/cp/cp17.pdf (last accessed; 16/09/12).

Financial Services Authority Handbook, *Code of Market Conduct (MAR 1)*, available at http://fsahandbook.info/FSA/html/handbook/MAR/1 (last accessed; 20/09/12).

'Fraud Trials Committee Report' (1986) HL Deb, 7: available at http://hansard.millbanksystems.com/lords/1986/feb/10/fraud-trials-committee-report (last accessed; 06/09/12).

G. P. Gilligan, *'Regulating Against White-Collar Crime in the Financial Services Sector'* (2000) 8(1) J.F.C, 7.

George Bray v. John Rawlinson Ford [1896] A.C. 44.

H. G. Manne, *'Insider Trading and Proprietary Rights in New Information'* (1985) 4(3) Cato Journal, 933.

H. Shefrin, *'Beyond Greed and Fear: Understanding Behavioural Finance and the Psychology of Investing'* (2002, Oxford University Press).

H. S. Houthakker and P. J. Williamson, *'The Economics of Financial Markets'* (1996, Oxford University Press).

Hall v. Cable and Wireless Plc [2011] B.C.C 543.

Hedley Byrne & Co. Ltd. Appellants; v. Heller & Partners Ltd. Respondents [1963] 3 W.L.R. 101.

http://europa.eu/rapid/pressReleasesAction.do?reference=IP/11/1217\&format=HTML\&aged=0\&language=EN\&guiLanguage=en (last accessed; 07/09/12).

http://europa.eu/rapid/pressReleasesAction.do?reference=IP/11/1218\&format=HTML\&aged=0\&language=EN\&guiLanguage=en (last accessed; 07/09/12).

http://fsahandbook.info/FSA/html/handbook/DISP/2/3 (last accessed; 10/09/12).

http://fsahandbook.info/FSA/html/handbook/DISP/2/7 (last accessed; 10/09/12).

http://fsahandbook.info/FSA/html/handbook/DISP/3/7 (last accessed; 10/09/12).

http://fsahandbook.info/FSA/html/handbook/MAR/Sch/5 (last accessed; 10/09/12).

http://fsahandbook.info/FSA/glossary-html/handbook/Glossary/R?definition=G974 (last accessed; 10/09/12).

http://www.efinancialnews.com/story/2010-09-29/lse-trading-update-uk (last accessed; 08/09/12).

http://www.financial-ombudsman.org.uk/ (last accessed: 10/09/12).

http://www.fsa.gov.uk/library/communication/pr/2012/060.shtml (last accessed; 09/09/12).

http://www.fsa.gov.uk/library/communication/pr/2012/082.shtml (last accessed 11/09/12).

http://www.fsa.gov.uk/pubs/annual/ar09_10/Section\%202.pdf (last accessed; 09/09/12).

http://www.fscs.org.uk/what-we-cover/questions-and-answers/ (last accessed; 18/09/12).

http://www.londonstockexchange.com/products-and-services/trading-services/guidetotradingservices.pdf (last accessed: 30/08/12).

http://www.publications.parliament.uk/pa/cm200607/cmpublic/cmpbfraud.htm (last accessed' 06/09/12).

http://www.sra.org.uk/solicitors/handbook/discproc/content.page (last accessed; 20/09/12).

I. B. Lee, *'Fairness and Insider Trading'* (2002) 1 Colum. Bus. L. Rev, 119.

J. Davis, *'Secrets of Success: Look to the History for how the Bubble will burst'* The Independent (London, 14 July 2004).

J. Dine, *'Criminal Law in the Company Context'* (1995, Dartmouth Publishing Company Limited).

J. Dine, *'The Comprehensive Review of Company Law: the Consultative Document'* (1998) 19(3) Comp. Law, 82.

J. Eeklaar and J. Bell, *'Oxford Essays in Jurisprudence'* (3rd Series, 1987, Oxford University Press).

J. E. Martin, *'Modern Equity'* (18th Ed. 2008, Sweet & Maxwell).

L. A. Stout, *'Are Stock Markets Costly Casinos? Disagreement, Market Failure, and Securities Regulation'* (1995) 81(3) Va. L. Rev, 611.

L. A. Stout, *'The Mechanisms of Market Inefficiency: an Introduction to New Finance'* (2003) 28(4) Journal of Corporation Law, 635.

L. D. Smith, *'The Law of Tracing'* (1997, Oxford University Press).

L. Gullifer and J. Payne, *'Corporate Finance Law: Principles and Policy'* (2011, Hart Publishing Ltd).

Loyds Bank Ltd v Bundy [1975] Q.B. 326.

M. Matravers, *'Justice and Punishment: The rationale of Coercion'* (2003, Oxford Scholarship Online).

M. S. Kenney, *'The role of national government in the restraint of global economic crime'* (1999) 7(2) J.F.C, 129.

Miza Mohamet Tackey v R. S. F. McBain [1912] A.C. 186.

N. Passas, *'Anomie and Corporate Deviance'* (1990) 14(2) Crime, Law and Social Change, 157.

P. Barnes, *'Insider Dealing and Market Abuse: the UKs Record on Enforcement'* [2010] MPRA Paper No. 25585: http://mpra.ub.uni-muenchen.de/25585/ (last accessed: 20/08/12).

P. Beresford and M. Chittenden, 'Super-rich reel from Eur200bn slump; Wealth Even Britain's billionaires cannot escape the pain of the economic squeeze. Philip Beresford and Maurice Chittenden find the big losers' *The Sunday Times* (London, 28 December 2008).

P. L. Davies, *'The European Community's Directive on Insider Dealing: From Company Law to Securities Markets Regulation'* [1991] Oxford J. Legal Stud, 92.

Pasley and Another v Freeman (1789) 3 Term Reports 51.

Percival v. Wright [1902] 2 Ch. 421.

R. J. Shiller, *'Measuring Bubble Expectations and Investor Confidence'* (2000) 1(1) Journal of Psychology and Financial Markets, Financial Markets, 49.

R. K. Merton, *'Social Structure and Anomie'* (1938) 3(5) American Sociological Review, 672.

R. Wright, *'Prosecution White Collar Crime – What's Going On?'* (1998) Amicus Curriae, 12. Available at: `http://sas-spa ce.sas.ac.uk/3969/1/1521-1830-1-SM.pdf` (last accessed: 01/09/12).

Re an enquiry under the Company Securities (Insider Dealing) Act 1985 [1988] 2 W.L.R. 33.

Regal (Hastings) Ltd v. Gulliver and Others [1967] 2 A.C. 134.

R v. Christopher McQuoid [2010] 1 Cr. App.R. (S.) 43.

R. v. Goodman [1992] B.C.C. 625.

S. Degeling and J. Edelman, *'Unjust Enrichment in Commercial Law'* (2008, Thomson Reuters (Professional) Australia Pty Limited t/a Lawbook Co.).

S. Gilotta, *'Disclosure in Securities Markets and the Firm's Need for Confidentiality: Theoretical Framework and Regulatory Analysis'* (2012) 13(1) E.B.O.R., 45.

S. Griffin, *'Company Law; Fundamental Principles'* (3rd Ed. 2000, Pearson Education Limited).

S. J. Grossman and J. E. Stiglitz, *'On the Impossibility of Infomrationally Efficient Markets'* (1980) 70(3) American Economic Review, 393.

S. P. Green, *'Cheating'* (2004) 23(2) Law & Phil, 135.

Sempra Metals Ltd (formerly Metallgesellschaft Ltd) v. Inland Revenue Commissioners and Another [2008] 1 A.C. 561.

T. Edmonds, *'Market Abuse Directive'*, House of Commons Library Publications, 15 June 2012.

T. Newburn, *'Criminolgy'* (2007, Willan Publishing).

The Council of the European Communities, Coordinating Regulations on Insider Dealing, 1989, Directive 89/592/EEC. Available at: http://www.esma.europa.eu/system/files/Dir_89_592.PDF (last accessed; 07/09/12).

The European Parliament and the Council of the European Union, Directive on Insider Dealing and Market Manipulation (Market Abuse) 2003, Directive 2003/6/EC: available at http://eur-lex.europa.eu/LexUriServ/LexUriServ.do?uri=OJ:L:2003:096:0016:0016:en:PDF (last accessed; 07/09/12).

W. V. H. Rogers, *'Tort'* (17th Ed. 2006, Sweet & Maxwell Limited).

William Derry, J. C. Wakefield, M. M. Moore, J. Pethick, and S. J. Wilde v Sir Henry William Peek, Baronet (1889) L.R. 14 App. Cas. 337.

William Smith v David Chadwick, John Oldfield Chadwick, Ebenezer Adamson, and Edwin Collier (1883-84) L.R. 9 App. Cas. 187.